NUMBERS FOR BEGINNERS

The Most Updated Crash Course to Numbers | Learn All the Functions, Macros, and Formulas to Become a Pro in 7 Days or Less

ANDREW BLAKE

TABLE OF CONTENTS

CHAPTER 1: INTRODUCTION

The Numbers app is a powerful spreadsheet application that lets you create, edit, and share spreadsheets on your iPhone or iPad. With Numbers, you can easily create beautiful charts and graphs, perform complex calculations, and easily share your work with others.

Numbers are the perfect tool for students, professionals, and anyone who needs to track and analyze data. Numbers is the perfect app for the job, whether you're tracking your expenses, keeping track of your fitness goals, or monitoring your investment portfolio.

With its intuitive interface and powerful features, Numbers is the perfect spreadsheet application for Mac, iPhone and iPad users.

The Numbers app for Apple products is a powerful tool that makes it easy to create beautiful spreadsheets. Here are some of its notable features:

A USER-FRIENDLY INTERFACE

One of the most notable features of the Numbers app is its user-friendly interface. The app is designed with a clean and simple layout, with menus and buttons that are easy to understand and navigate. This makes it easy for users, even those who have never used the app before, to create and edit spreadsheets quickly and efficiently.

The interface of the Numbers app is organized into several sections, including the main menu, the toolbar, and the sidebar. The main menu provides access to all the main features of the app, such as formatting, chart creation, and formula creation. The toolbar provides quick access to commonly used tools, such as font and cell formatting, and the sidebar provides access to additional features, such as tables and media.

The app also has a consistent design across all of its features, which makes it easy for users to learn and use new features quickly. The various menus and options are easy to understand and are labeled clearly, so users can easily find the features they need.

Another aspect of the user-friendly interface is the ability to customize the layout to suit individual preferences. Users can customize the toolbar to include only the tools they need, which makes the app more efficient to use. Additionally, users can customize the appearance of the app, including the background color and font style.

AN ARRAY OF CUSTOMIZABLE TEMPLATES

The templates provided by Numbers are fully customizable, allowing users to edit the design and structure of the template to suit their specific needs. Users can change the font, color scheme, and layout of the template, as well as add or remove tables, charts, and other data structures.

In addition to pre-designed templates, Numbers also provides users with the ability to create custom templates. Users can create a custom template by selecting a blank spreadsheet and adding their own tables, charts, and other data structures. This feature is useful for users who have specific needs that are not met by the pre-designed templates.

One of the most significant advantages of the template feature in Numbers is that it saves time and effort. Users can select a pre-designed template and customize it to suit their needs, without having to spend hours designing the spreadsheet from scratch. This feature is especially useful for users who need to create a spreadsheet quickly or who are not experienced in spreadsheet design.

Another benefit of the template feature is that it ensures consistency in design and structure. By using a pre-designed template, users can ensure that their spreadsheet follows a consistent layout and design, which makes it easier to read and understand.

CUSTOMIZABLE CELLS

Another notable feature of the Numbers app is its ability to customize individual cells within a spreadsheet. One of the most useful cell customization features in Numbers is the ability to format text. Users can adjust the font style, size, and color of text within individual cells or groups of cells. They can also format numbers to display as currency, percentage, or decimal, depending on their preference.

Numbers also allows users to adjust the borders around individual cells or groups of cells. Users can adjust the thickness and color of the borders, as well as add or remove individual borders. This feature is useful for creating tables or grids within a spreadsheet and making them more visually appealing.

Another powerful cell customization feature in Numbers is the ability to apply conditional formatting to specific cells. This feature allows users to set specific formatting rules based on the values within the cell. For example, users can set a rule to highlight any cell that contains a certain value or a value that falls within a specific range.

In addition to formatting text, borders, and applying conditional formatting, Numbers also allows users to add or delete rows and columns within a spreadsheet. This feature is useful for adjusting the layout of a spreadsheet or for adding new data to an existing spreadsheet.

ADVANCED FORMULAS AND FUNCTIONS

The Numbers app provides advanced formulas and functions that allow users to perform complex calculations quickly and easily. These formulas and functions are designed to help users save time and increase accuracy in their spreadsheets, making the app an essential tool for professionals who need to perform calculations regularly.

One of the most useful advanced formulas in Numbers is the SUMIF function. This function allows users to sum a range of cells that meet specific criteria. For example, users can use this function to sum all the sales that were made in a specific month or by a specific salesperson.

Another powerful formula in Numbers is the VLOOKUP function. This function allows users to find and retrieve data from a specific range of cells based on a specific value. For example, users can use this function to retrieve a customer's contact information based on their name or customer ID.

The Numbers app also includes a range of statistical functions, such as AVERAGE, STDEV, and COUNT. These functions are designed to help users analyze data and make informed decisions based on their findings.

In addition to the built-in formulas and functions, Numbers also allows users to create their own custom formulas. This feature is beneficial for users who need to perform calculations that are not included in the app's built-in formulas.

CHARTS AND GRAPHS

As you create spreadsheets in the Numbers app, you may want to use charts and graphs to visualize your data. Charts and graphs can assist in making your data easier to comprehend and interpret.

Numerous charts and graphs are available in Numbers, so selecting the right one for your data is critical. In general, you should use a graph or chart when you have numerical data that you want to visualize.

Some common reasons to use charts and graphs in Numbers include:

- To compare two or more sets of data
- To spot trends in your data
- To see relationships between different variables
- To make your data more understandable

When choosing a chart or graph, you must consider the type of data you have and what you want to accomplish with it. For example, if you have data that changes over time, you may want to use a line graph. A bar chart may be better if you want to compare different data sets.

Once you've selected the right chart or graph, you can use the built-in tools in Numbers to customize it to your liking.

If you're unsure which chart or graph to use, try experimenting with different options until you find one that works best for your data.

Charts and graphs are a great way to see patterns and trends in your data and can be helpful in understanding complex information. The Numbers app offers various charts and graphs, including line graphs, bar graphs, pie charts, and scatter plots.

You can create a wide range of charts and graphs in the Numbers app on your Apple device. Here are a few of the most well-known:

- **Bar Chart**: A bar chart is similar to a column chart, but the bars are horizontal instead of vertical. It is often used to compare data across different categories.
- **Pie Chart**: A pie chart is used to show how different components contribute to a whole. It is often used to display the percentage of revenue that comes from different product lines or the proportion of the budget that is allocated to different departments.
- **Line Graph**: Is used to show trends in data over time. It is often used to display stock prices, weather patterns, and other data that changes over time.
- **Area Graph**: Is used to show changes in data over time, but the area under the line is shaded to emphasize the cumulative values. It is often used to display sales figures or website traffic over time.
- **Scatter Plot**: Is used to show the relationship between two variables. It is often used to display data from scientific experiments, such as the relationship between temperature and pressure.

As you can see, the Numbers app provides users with a wide range of well-known charts and graphs that can be used to visualize data effectively. By choosing the right chart or graph for their data and customizing its appearance, users can communicate their findings effectively and make informed decisions based on their data. Experiment with different types to see which is best for your data set.

COMPATIBILITY WITH OTHER APPLE PRODUCTS

The Numbers app is designed to be fully compatible with other Apple products, including Mac computers, iPhones, and iPads. This means that users can seamlessly move between different Apple devices and continue working on their spreadsheets without interruption.

For example, a user can start working on a Numbers spreadsheet on their Mac computer, save it to iCloud, and then continue working on it on their iPhone or iPad. Any changes made on one device will be automatically synced to the other devices, ensuring that the user always has the most up-to-date version of their spreadsheet.

In addition to seamless syncing between devices, Numbers is also fully compatible with other Apple apps, such as Pages and Keynote. This means that users can easily import data from Numbers into Pages or Keynote to create reports, presentations, and other documents.

Another way that Numbers is compatible with other Apple products is through its support for Apple Pencil. Users can use an Apple Pencil to draw and write directly on their spreadsheets, which is particularly useful for adding annotations, highlighting important data points, or making calculations by hand.

The Numbers app has features to help you get the most out of your data. Here's a quick rundown of some of the things you can do:

- View and edit your data in a spreadsheet-like interface
- Apply formulas to perform calculations on your data
- Create charts and graphs for a better presentation of your statistics
- Share your data with others via email or social media
- Save your data as a CSV file to use in other apps.

CHAPTER 2: CREATING AND CUSTOMIZING FORMS IN NUMBERS

You might want to create a custom form in Numbers for many reasons. Perhaps you need a specific format for data entry or want to create a survey that can be easily shared and completed online. For this reason, creating a custom form in Numbers is easy.

Creating a custom form in Numbers starts with choosing the type of form you want to create. There are three main forms: data entry, questionnaires, and surveys.

Data entry forms are designed for easy data entry. They typically have a simple layout with fields for each piece of information you want to collect.

Questionnaires are similar to data entry forms but include questions that help gather information about a specific topic.

Surveys are forms that are designed to be completed by a large number of people. They typically include questions about various topics and can be distributed online or in person.

Once you've chosen the type of form you want to create, you can start customizing it to fit your needs. For example, you can add or delete fields, change the order of fields, or add custom questions.

You can also customize the look of your form by changing the colors, fonts, and layout. And if you're creating a survey, you can add a logo or image to the form.

Creating a custom form in Numbers is a great way to collect data specific to your needs. And with a little bit of customization, you can create a form that's uniquely yours.

HOW TO CREATE A FORM IN NUMBERS

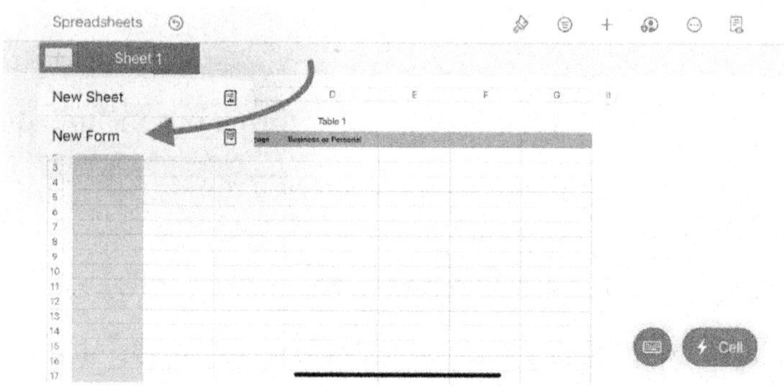

Creating a form in Numbers is a simple process that you can complete in just a few steps.

1. Open the Numbers app on your Mac.
2. Click on "New Document" to create a new spreadsheet.
3. From the template chooser, select the "Forms" category on the left-hand side.
4. Choose a form template that best fits your needs, or click "Blank" to create a custom form from scratch.
5. Start by customizing the form by adding fields, such as text boxes, checkboxes, radio buttons, or drop-down menus, using the "Add Field" button located in the top-right corner of the screen.
6. Use the "Inspector" panel to customize the form's appearance and behavior, such as the font, color, and formatting of the fields.

7. Once you have added all the fields you need, you can share your form by clicking the "Share" button in the top-right corner of the screen, selecting a sharing option, and sending the link to your recipients.

That's all there is to it! Creating a form in Numbers is quick and easy and can be a great way to collect information from people. Give it a try today.

HOW TO CUSTOMIZE A FORM IN NUMBERS

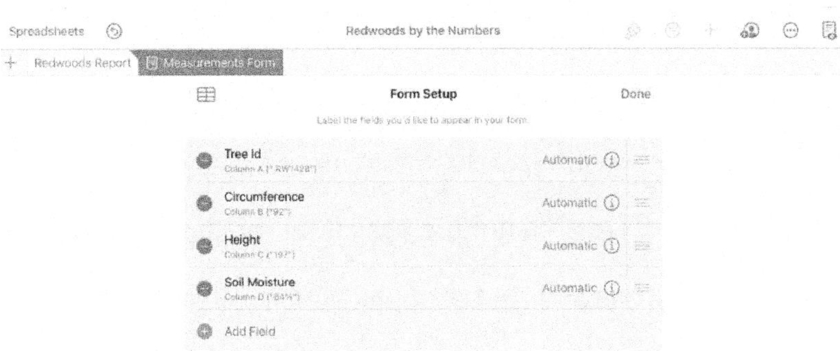

In Numbers, you can customize your forms to suit your needs better. To do this, follow these steps:

1. Open the Numbers app and create a new form by selecting the "Blank" template from the list of available templates.
2. Once the form is open, click on the "Fields" button in the top right corner of the screen. This will display a list of available fields that can be added to the form.
3. To add a field to the form, simply drag and drop it from the list of available fields onto the form. Users can add as many fields as they need to capture all of the information they require.
4. To customize the appearance of the form, users can use the formatting tools in the "Style" tab. This allows users to change the font, color, and other visual elements of the form to make it more visually appealing and easier to read.
5. To further customize the form, users can add images or other visual elements. To do this, select the "Media" button and then select the image or other media element that you want to add to the form.
6. Once the form is complete, users can share it with others by clicking on the "Share" button in the top right corner of the screen. This will allow users to send the form via email, message, or other means.

HOW TO USE CONDITIONAL FORMATTING IN FORM

Conditional formatting is a useful feature in Numbers that allows you to highlight important data in your forms automatically. This can help you to draw attention to specific data, making it easier to understand and analyze. Here's a guide on how to use conditional formatting in forms in Numbers:

1. Open the form that you want to add conditional formatting to in Numbers.
2. Select the cells that you want to apply conditional formatting to.
3. Click on the "Format" button in the top-right corner of the screen, then click on "Conditional Highlighting" from the dropdown menu.
4. Choose the type of conditional formatting that you want to apply. You can choose from a variety of options, including "Greater Than," "Less Than," "Between," and "Text Contains."
5. Set the formatting options for the selected cells. For example, if you choose the "Greater Than" option, you can set a threshold value and a color for cells that are greater than that value.
6. Click the "Apply" button to apply the conditional formatting to the selected cells.

HOW TO TEST A FORM

If you're a beginner and want to test forms in Numbers, here are some simple steps to follow:

- Preview the form: First, open the form you want to test and click on the "Preview" button located in the top-right corner of the screen. This will allow you to see what the form looks like to someone who will be filling it out.
- Test each field: Next, fill out each field to make sure it works correctly. Try entering different types of data, such as numbers, text, and dates, and see if the form accepts them. If any fields have validation rules, test those rules to make sure they work correctly.
- Submit the form: Once you have filled out the form, click on the "Submit" button to see if the form submits the data as expected. If the form is set up to send a confirmation email or message, check to make sure that you receive it.
- Review the data: After submitting the form, go to the "Responses" tab to see if the data was saved correctly. Check to make sure that all the data you entered is there and that it was saved in the correct format.
- Make adjustments: If you find any issues or errors during testing, make adjustments to the form as needed. You can make changes to the form layout, fields, and validation rules to improve the user experience.

Testing forms in Numbers is an essential step to ensure that the forms work as expected and that they provide a smooth user experience. By following these steps, you can test your forms in Numbers and make sure that they are functional, easy to use, and user-friendly.

HOW TO SHARE YOUR FORM IN NUMBERS

You can use the Share feature in Numbers when you want to share your form with others. It will allow you to share your form as a PDF or spreadsheet. To share your form:

1. Open the form that you want to share in Numbers.
2. Click on the "Share" button in the top-right corner of the screen. This will open the sharing options.
3. Select the method of sharing that you want to use. You can choose to share the form via email, message, or other means.
4. If you choose to share the form via email or message, enter the email or phone number of the recipient in the appropriate field. You can also add a message to the recipient.
5. Choose the format of the form that you want to share. You can choose to share the form in Numbers, Excel, or PDF format.
6. Click the "Share" button to send the form to the recipient.

Choose where you want to share your form. You can share it via email, Messages, Airdrop, or any other compatible app on your device.

TIPS FOR CREATING AND CUSTOMIZING FORMS IN NUMBER

Creating and customizing forms in Numbers can be an easy and straightforward process if you keep a few tips in mind. Here are some tips for creating and customizing forms in Numbers:

1. **Choose the right form template:** Numbers provides a variety of templates to choose from. Select the template that is best suited for your specific needs. This can help you save time and create forms that are both functional and visually appealing.
2. **Customize your form:** Customize the form to include fields and information that you require. This can help you capture all the necessary information in one place.
3. **Preview your form:** Before sharing your form with others, preview it to ensure that it looks the way you want it to. This can help you catch any errors or formatting issues before it is shared.
4. **Share your form:** Once your form is complete, you can share it with others. Numbers provides various options for sharing your form, such as sending it via email, message, or printing it.
5. **Use consistent formatting:** Consistency in formatting can help to make your form more professional and easier to read. Use the same font and font size throughout the form, and make sure that the fields are properly aligned.
6. **Keep it simple:** A simple form is often more effective than a complex one. Keep your form as simple as possible by only including the necessary fields and information.

7. **Use conditional formatting:** Use conditional formatting to highlight important information in your form. This can help to draw attention to specific fields, making it easier for users to quickly understand the information presented.
8. **Test the form:** Before sharing the form with others, test it to ensure that it is working as intended. This can help you to catch any errors or issues with the form before it is shared.
9. **Consider using automation:** Numbers provides a variety of automation options that can help to streamline the form creation process. Consider using automation to speed up data entry or to perform calculations automatically.

By following these additional tips, you can create forms in Numbers that are effective, efficient, and easy to use. By keeping the form simple, using consistent formatting, and testing the form before sharing it, you can ensure that the form meets your needs and is easy for others to use.

CHAPTER 3: ANALYZING DATA WITH PIVOT TABLES

WHAT IS A PIVOT TABLE?

A pivot table allows one to summarize and analyze data in Apple Numbers. You can use pivot tables to calculate summaries, find trends, and even spot outliers in your data. Pivot tables are simple to make and can be helpful to any Numbers spreadsheet.

You might want to use a pivot table in Apple Numbers for many reasons. Perhaps you have a large dataset to summarize, or you want to look for trends in your data. Pivot tables can be an invaluable tool for any Numbers user. Pivot tables are used for data analysis, allowing you to summarize and compare large amounts of data quickly. The Numbers app for Apple devices makes it easy to create and use pivot tables. A pivot table can be extremely useful when working with large amounts of data. They also allow you to quickly summarize and compare large amounts of data without wading through all the details.

CREATING PIVOT TABLES IN NUMBERS

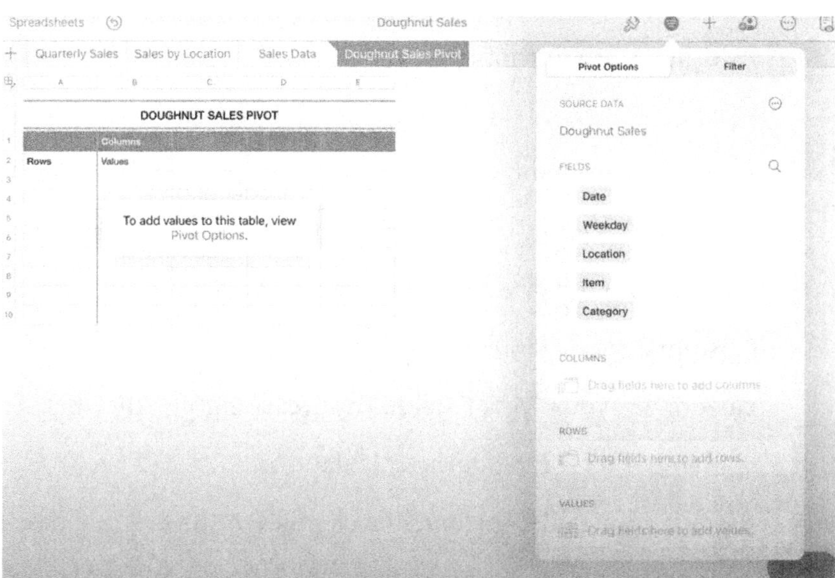

Pivot tables are a powerful tool for analyzing large data sets and identifying trends and patterns. In Numbers, creating pivot tables is a straightforward process that can be done in just a few steps. Here's how to create pivot tables in Numbers:

- Open your spreadsheet: First, open the Numbers spreadsheet that contains the data you want to analyze.
- Select your data: Next, select the data you want to include in your pivot table. Make sure that your data is organized in columns and rows, with each column containing a header.
- Create a new table: After selecting your data, go to the "Table" menu and select "New Table". This will create a new table in your spreadsheet.
- Add fields to your table: In the new table, you'll see a "Fields" pane on the right side of the screen. Drag the headers of the columns you want to include in your pivot table into the "Rows" or "Columns" area of the Fields pane. You can also drag headers into the "Values" area to summarize your data.
- Customize your table: Once you've added your fields, you can customize your pivot table by rearranging the headers, applying filters, and adding calculations.
- Refresh your table: If you make changes to the original data in your spreadsheet, you'll need to refresh your pivot table to see the changes. To do this, click on the "Refresh" button in the top-left corner of your pivot table.

By following these steps, you can create pivot tables in Numbers and use them to analyze and summarize your data. Pivot tables are a great way to get a high-level view of your data and identify trends and patterns that might be difficult to see otherwise. With Numbers, creating pivot tables is easy and can be done in just a few simple steps.

USING PIVOT TABLES TO IDENTIFY TRENDS

Now that we know how to make a pivot table, let's see how we can use it to find trends. There are several approaches to this, including using pivot charts, filters, and sorts.

One way to use pivot tables to find trends is to create a pivot chart. After creating your pivot table, choose "Chart" from the Insert menu, and select "Line" as the chart type. The resulting line chart will show you how your data has changed over time and can be helpful for spotting trends. For example, you might notice that your sales have been increasing steadily over the past few months.

Another approach is to use the filter feature. With your pivot table selected, go to the Data menu and select "Filter." In the resulting dialog box, you can choose which data to include in your pivot table. For example, you might only want to include data from the past year. Filtering your data can be helpful for spotting trends that might not be immediately obvious.

Lastly, you can use Numbers' sort feature to find trends. With your pivot table selected, go to the Data menu and select "Sort." You can choose how you will sort your data in the resulting dialog box. Sorting your data by a particular field can help spot trends, such as seasonal trends. For example, you might see that sales are higher in the summer than in the winter.

Let's say you have a pivot table that shows the number of products sold by month, and you want to identify which months have seen the highest sales. Here's how each approach could be used:

- Pivot chart: You create a pivot chart and notice that sales have increased steadily over the past few months, with the highest sales occurring in the most recent month.
- Filter: You use the filter feature to only show data from the last six months, and notice that sales have been consistently high in the past two months.
- Sort: You sort the data by month and see that sales are highest in July and August, which are the summer months.

By using these methods to find trends in your data, you can gain valuable insights and make informed decisions. Pivot tables are a great tool for analyzing data, and using these features in Numbers makes it easy to spot trends that might otherwise go unnoticed.

BEST PRACTICES FOR EFFECTIVE PIVOT TABLE USAGE

While the basic steps of creating a pivot table in Numbers are relatively straightforward, there are some best practices you can follow to make your pivot tables more effective. Here are some tips for using pivot tables in Numbers:

- Start with well-organized data: Before creating a pivot table, make sure that your data is well-organized, with clear headers and consistent formatting. This will make it easier to create a pivot table that accurately reflects your data.
- Choose the right type of pivot table: There are several types of pivot tables to choose from, including table, column, row, and page. Choose the type of pivot table that best suits your needs, based on the type of data you have and the questions you want to answer.
- Use filters to refine your data: Filters allow you to limit the data displayed in your pivot table based on specific criteria. This can help you focus on a particular subset of your data, making it easier to spot trends or patterns.
- Format your pivot table: Once you have created your pivot table, take the time to format it in a way that is easy to read and understand. Use bold fonts, colors, and borders to make your pivot table stand out on the page.

- Update your pivot table regularly: If your data changes frequently, make sure to update your pivot table regularly to reflect the latest information. This will ensure that you always have the most accurate and up-to-date information.

For example, suppose you have a table that shows the sales figures for different products in different regions. By using a pivot table, you can quickly see which products are selling the most and in which regions. You could use a filter to limit the data to a specific region, or you could sort the data by product to see which products are the most popular.

TROUBLESHOOTING COMMON PIVOT TABLE ISSUES

While pivot tables in Numbers can be a powerful tool for data analysis, there can be instances where you may encounter issues. Here are some common pivot table issues you may encounter and troubleshooting tips to help resolve them:

1. Incorrect Data: If you notice that your pivot table is not displaying accurate data, double-check your source data to make sure it is correct. Additionally, check your pivot table settings to ensure they are configured properly.
2. Missing Data: If you notice that certain data is missing from your pivot table, check to make sure that the relevant columns and rows are included in your source data. Also, make sure that the field headers in your source data match the headers in your pivot table.
3. Incorrect Pivot Table Settings: If your pivot table is not displaying the data you expect, check to make sure that your pivot table settings are configured correctly. You can do this by clicking on the pivot table and checking the "Pivot Table Editor" window.
4. Data is not Refreshing: If your pivot table is not updating with new data, make sure that automatic updates are turned on. You can do this by going to the "Pivot Table Editor" and selecting "Refresh Data." You can also manually refresh your pivot table by selecting "Refresh Table" from the "Data" menu.
5. Large Data Sets: If you have a large amount of data in your pivot table, it may take longer to load or update. Consider optimizing your data by removing unnecessary columns or rows.

By troubleshooting these common pivot table issues, you can ensure that your pivot tables in Numbers are accurately displaying your data and providing valuable insights.

Organize Your Data

Make sure that your data is organized correctly. Pivot tables require that your data be organized in a specific way to work properly. If your data is not organized correctly, the pivot table will not be able to interpret it correctly.

Check for Blank Cells

Next, check to see any blank cells in your data. Blank cells can cause problems with pivot tables, so it's important to ensure that all your data is entered correctly. Finally, check your pivot table's settings to ensure everything is set up correctly. You can always contact Numbers support for help if you're still having trouble.

You should be able to troubleshoot any pivot table issues using these tips. Have fun pivoting!

FAQS ABOUT PIVOT TABLES

Q: How do I change the Pivot Table layout in Numbers?

A: To change the layout of a pivot table in Numbers, first click the Layout tab. Then use the options in the Pivot Table Layout section to specify how you want your pivot table to look. For example, you can choose whether to show or hide subtotals and grand totals, or you can choose to display data in a tabular or compact form.

Q: How do I filter data in a Pivot Table in Numbers?

A: To filter data in a pivot table in Numbers, first click the Data tab. Then use the options in the Pivot Table Data section to specify which data you want to include in your pivot table. For example, you can choose to only show data for a specific period or a specific category.

Q: How do I format a Pivot Table in Numbers?

A: First, click the Format tab to format a pivot table in Numbers. Then use the options in the Pivot Table Format section to specify how you want your pivot table to look. You can, for example, change the number format or the font style and size. You can add borders or background colors to your pivot table using the options in this section.

Q: How do I print a Pivot Table in Numbers?

A: To print a pivot table in Numbers, first click the File tab. Then select Print from the drop-down menu. Next, choose how you want your pivot table to be printed. For example, you can print only the data or the pivot table, including the field list and header. Finally, click the Print button.

CHAPTER 4: VISUALIZING DATA WITH RADAR CHARTS

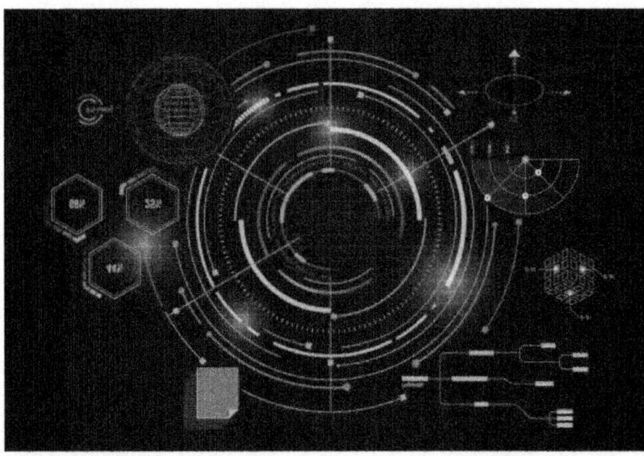

WHAT IS A RADAR CHART?

Radar charts are mainly used to compare data sets and visualize relationships between them. You can use them to show how different items in a data set relate to or compare two or more data sets.

Radar charts are composed of a series of connected lines, called radii, which originate from a common center point. The length of each line represents the value of the item to which it is connected. The lines are arranged to form a circle, or radii, with the center point in the middle.

Radar charts are a great way to see how data sets compare. You can use them to compare items in a data set or two or more data sets. Radar charts are also a good way to see relationships between different items in a data set

NUMBERS APP AND RADAR CHART

The numbers app is a powerful tool to help you create sophisticated charts and graphs. One type of chart you may want to use is a radar chart. Radar charts are useful for visualizing data that has multiple variables. For example, a radar chart can be used to compare the performance of two different athletes.

Radar charts are similar to line graphs but have a few key differences. First, radar charts show data points that are connected by lines. It makes it easy to see patterns and relationships between data points. Second, you can use radar charts to show data over time. It is helpful if you want to track an athlete's progress or compare the performance of two athletes over time.

If you're looking for a way to visualize data more sophisticatedly, consider using a radar chart in Numbers App. Radar charts can help you see relationships and patterns that you may not be able to see with other types of charts.

CREATING RADAR CHARTS IN NUMBERS

You can use radar charts to compare two or more data sets.

1. Click on the "Charts" button in the toolbar and choose "Radar" from the list of chart types.
2. A default radar chart will be created with your data. You can now customize the chart by clicking on it and using the "Chart" and "Format" tabs in the sidebar.
3. In the "Chart" tab, you can adjust settings like the chart title, data labels, and grid lines. In the "Format" tab, you can change the appearance of the chart, including colors, fonts, and the chart style.
4. If you need to add or remove data from your chart, simply select the chart and click on the "Chart Data" button in the toolbar. From there, you can add or remove data from your chart as needed.
5. Finally, you can adjust the layout of your chart by selecting it and using the green dots that appear around the chart to resize and position it on your sheet.
6. Click the Save button to save changes.

INTERPRETING RADAR CHART

Radar charts help to visualize data but can be tricky to interpret. Here are a few tips to help you make the most of your radar chart:

Look at the Overall Shape of the Data

When looking at a radar chart, the overall shape of the data is what you should focus on. It will give you an idea of the general trends and patterns in the data. Specifically, look for clusters of data points and any outlier points. These can give you insights into the factors most important to the data set.

To interpret a radar chart, start by looking at the overall shape of the data. If the data is clustered together, this indicates that there is a strong relationship between the variables. The relationship between the variables is weak if the data is spread out. You can also look at the individual data points to see any outliers.

Next, compare the different data sets on the radar chart. Look for similarities and differences in the shapes of the data sets. It can give an insight into the relationship between the variables. Finally, compare the data sets to any external data that you have. It can help you understand the data's context and see if there are any trends you can identify.

You can also compare different data sets to look for trends. Finally, you can compare the data to external data to understand the context of the data.

Pay Attention to the Axes

When reading a radar chart, it is important to pay attention to the axes. The axes represent the different variables that are being compared. The length of each line represents the value of that variable.

So, if you are looking at a radar chart comparing the average temperatures of two cities, the city with the long line would be the warmer city.

It is also necessary to pay attention to the scale of each axis. The scale will tell you how big the difference is between the two values. For example, if the scale goes from 0 to 100, then a difference of 50 would be significant, but if the scale only goes from 0 to 10, that difference of 50 would not be as substantial.

When looking at a radar chart, pay attention to the axes and the scale to interpret the data correctly.

Each axis represents a different data point, so make sure you know what each one represents. Finally, don't forget to label your axes! It will help you and others interpret the data more efficiently.

Look for Patterns in the Individual Data Points

When looking at a radar chart, you should look for patterns in the individual data points. Do any of the points form a line? Are any of the points particularly far from the others?

Once you've identified any patterns, you can start to interpret what they mean. For example, if all of the points form a line, that could indicate that the data is linear. If one point is far from the others, that could indicate an outlier.

Keep in mind that no one correct interpretation of a radar chart exists. The important thing is to look for patterns and then think about what those patterns could mean.

CUSTOMIZING RADAR CHARTS IN NUMBERS

Customizing radar charts in Numbers can help to make your data more understandable and visually appealing. Here are some ways you can customize radar charts:

1. Change the Chart Type: By default, a radar chart is set to show each data series as a line. However, you can change the chart type to show each data series as a filled shape. To do this, select the chart, go to the Format sidebar, and choose the "Chart" tab. Then, choose "Filled" from the "Line Type" drop-down menu.

2. Adjust the Scale: Depending on your data, you may need to adjust the scale of the radar chart. To do this, select the chart and go to the Format sidebar. Choose the "Axes" tab, and then choose "Primary Radial" from the drop-down menu. From there, you can adjust the minimum, maximum, and interval values for the scale.
3. Change the Data Series Colors: By default, Numbers assigns different colors to each data series in a radar chart. However, you may want to change these colors to better match your presentation or branding. To do this, select the chart and go to the Format sidebar. Choose the "Chart" tab, and then choose "Series" from the drop-down menu. From there, you can choose a new color for each data series.
4. Add Data Labels: To make your radar chart more readable, you may want to add data labels to each data point. To do this, select the chart and go to the Format sidebar. Choose the "Chart" tab, and then choose "Data Labels" from the drop-down menu. From there, you can choose to show the values or percentages for each data point.
5. Customize the Legend: By default, Numbers displays a legend for each data series in a radar chart. However, you may want to customize the legend to better match your presentation or branding. To do this, select the chart and go to the Format sidebar. Choose the "Chart" tab, and then choose "Legend" from the drop-down menu. From there, you can customize the font, size, and position of the legend.

6. Add Gridlines: Gridlines can help to make your radar chart more readable and understandable. To add gridlines to a radar chart, select the chart and go to the Format sidebar. Choose the "Chart" tab, and then choose "Gridlines" from the drop-down menu. From there, you can choose to show or hide the gridlines, and customize the style and color of the lines.

ADVANTAGES OF USING RADAR CHARTS

Radar charts are a great way to visualize data. They can be used to show trends over time or to compare different data sets. Radar charts are also easy to read and understand, making them a valuable tool for decision-makers.

There are many advantages to using radar charts in Numbers. Here are just a few:

Radar Charts are Easy to Understand

Radar charts are easy to understand and can be a valuable tool for decision-making. They are handy for comparing data sets that have different ranges. For example, you can easily use a radar chart to compare your company's sales figures for the past year. The chart would show how each month's sales compared to the others, and you could quickly see which months were the best and worst performers.

You can also use radar charts to track progress. For example, you could track your team's sales figures month-by-month. It would allow you to see how the team performs and identify trends.

Radar charts are a great option if you're looking for a way to compare data sets and see how they relate. They're easy to understand and can be a valuable tool for decision-making.

You can use Radar Charts to Compare Different Data Sets

You can use radar charts to see how different groups of people or different types of data compare. You can use radar charts to compare anything from age groups to income levels.

Radar charts are handy for comparing data with many different variables. For example, you could use a radar chart to compare the age, income, and education level of two different groups of people.

Radar charts are also an excellent way to visualize data that changes over time. You can use them to see how a group of people's age, income, and education level have changed over time.

Radar Charts are a Valuable Tool for Decision-Makers

Radar charts in Numbers are a valuable tool for decision-makers. They provide an easy way to compare data points and make informed decisions. You can use radar charts to track progress over time, compare data sets, or make forecasts. When used correctly, radar charts can be an invaluable asset in the decision-making process.

Radar charts are created by plotting data points on a two-dimensional graph. The data points are connected to form a polygon. The shape of the polygon will vary depending on the plotted data points. You can use radar charts to track progress over time, compare data sets, or make forecasts.

When used correctly, radar charts can be an invaluable asset in the decision-making process. They provide an easy way to compare data points and make informed decisions. However, radar charts can also be misleading if not used correctly. It is crucial to understand how radar charts work before making decisions.

Radar Charts are a Great Way to Visualize Data

Radar charts are of great help in visualizing data. They can be used to show how different items compare to one another or to show how a single item changes over time.

Radar charts are created by plotting data points on a grid and then connecting the dots to create a polygon. You can use the size of the polygons to visualize the data, with larger polygons representing larger values.

These are great tools for visualizing data and showing how different items compare or how a single item changes over time.

If you're looking for a way to visualize your data better, consider using radar charts in Numbers. You'll be glad you did!

DISADVANTAGES OF USING RADAR CHARTS

Radar charts have a few disadvantages that you should consider before using them.

Difficulty in Reading

Radar charts are often criticized for being difficult to read and interpret. It is because the various data points are spread out evenly around the perimeter of the chart, making it hard to compare them side by side. In addition, the lines connecting the data points can be confusing and make it difficult to see relationships between different data sets.

Can be Misleading

Radar charts are a great way to compare data sets, but they can also be misleading. When using radar charts, it's important to remember that the data points' angles can distort the data. For example, if two data sets have the same value for one data point but different values for another, the data set with the higher value will appear further away from the center of the chart. It can be misleading, and it's essential to be aware of this when interpreting data from a radar chart.

Radar charts can also be difficult to read because all data points appear to be the same distance from the center. It is why it's often helpful to use colors or different shapes to distinguish between different data sets on a radar chart.

Not Well-Suited for Comparing More Than Two Data Sets

Radar charts are not well suited for comparing more than two data sets in Numbers. They can often be misleading when comparing three or more data sets. It is because the shape of the radar chart changes as more data sets are added, making it difficult to accurately compare the data sets' relative sizes.

Overall, radar charts are a great tool for comparing data sets, but it's essential to be aware of their limitations. If you're not careful, radar charts can be misleading. However, if you keep these things in mind, radar charts can be a great way to visualize data.

CHAPTER 5: CONVERTING HANDWRITING TO TEXT IN NUMBERS

As you may know, Numbers is a spreadsheet application part of the iWork suite of productivity applications. While it is primarily designed for working with numbers and data, it also has some great features for working with text. One of these features is the ability to turn handwriting into text.

It can be a great way to enter data into a spreadsheet if you don't have a keyboard handy or prefer to write instead of type. It can also be helpful for quickly jotting down notes or ideas.

You can use the Turning handwriting into text feature in Numbers in a few different ways. You can use it to quickly enter data into a spreadsheet or convert a handwritten note into text that you can edit.

If you're using the feature to enter data into a spreadsheet, you can write the data in the cells where you want it to appear. Handwriting recognition will convert your handwriting into text and enter it into the cell.

If you're using the feature to convert a handwritten note into editable text, you can write the note in any blank area of the Numbers document. When you're finished, tap the Convert button, and handwriting recognition will convert your handwriting into text. The text will appear in a new text box that you can move and resize as needed. You can edit the text as you would any other text in Numbers.

Turning handwriting into text can be a great way to quickly enter data into a Numbers spreadsheet or convert a handwritten note into editable text.

BENEFITS OF CONVERTING HANDWRITING TO TEXT

Here are the listed reasons why you might want to turn handwritten text into typed text in Numbers:

- You've been given a document only available in handwritten form.
- You've taken some notes by hand and want to type them up.
- You want to make your handwritten text more legible.
- You want to make searching for specific text within a handwritten document easier.
- You want to save your handwritten text as a PDF or other format.

These are valid reasons why you might want to turn handwritten text into typed text in Numbers. And luckily, doing so is a relatively simple process.

CONVERTING HANDWRITING TO TEXT WITH KEYBOARD SHORTCUTS

Converting handwriting to text is a useful feature in Numbers that can save you time and make your data more organized. One way to do this is by using keyboard shortcuts. Here's how to convert handwriting to text with keyboard shortcuts in Numbers:

1. First, open the Numbers app and select the cell that contains the handwritten text you want to convert.

2. Next, click on the cell to make it active, and then press the "Control" and "Command" keys simultaneously.
3. While holding down the "Control" and "Command" keys, tap the spacebar on your keyboard. This will open the "Dictation" tool in Numbers.
4. Once the "Dictation" tool is open, move your cursor over the handwritten text and click on it. The tool will then begin converting the handwriting to text.
5. When the conversion is complete, you can edit the text as needed.

Using keyboard shortcuts to convert handwriting to text is a quick and easy way to get your handwritten data into a digital format. With just a few keystrokes, you can have your data ready to be analyzed or shared.

CONVERTING HANDWRITING TO TEXT WITH TOUCH BAR

In Numbers for Mac, you can quickly use the Touch Bar to convert handwriting to text. Here's how:

1. First, open the Numbers app and select the cell that contains the handwritten text you want to convert.
2. Next, click on the cell to make it active, and then tap the "Input Source" button on the Touch Bar. This button looks like a globe with a pen.

3. In the input source options that appear on the Touch Bar, select "Convert to Text." This will open the "Dictation" tool in Numbers.
4. Once the "Dictation" tool is open, move your cursor over the handwritten text and click on it. The tool will then begin converting the handwriting to text.
5. When the conversion is complete, you can edit the text as needed.

The text you entered will appear in the cell. If you make a mistake, tap to delete it, then start again.

You can also use the Touch Bar to convert images of handwritten text into editable text. Here's how:

1. Open the Numbers app and select the cell that contains the image of the handwritten text you want to convert.
2. Tap on the cell to make it active, and then look for the "Convert Handwriting" button on the Touch Bar.
3. Tap on the "Convert Handwriting" button to activate the feature.
4. The Touch Bar will then display a preview of the converted text.
5. If you're satisfied with the conversion, simply click on the text preview to insert it into the cell.
6. You can then edit the text as needed.

The text you entered will appear in the cell. If you make a mistake, tap to delete it, then start again.

BEST PRACTICES FOR ACCURATE TEXT CONVERSION

The Conversion Process is not Perfect

As we all know, the conversion process is not perfect when converting handwriting to text in Numbers. Inevitably, some of the original content will be lost or changed. It can be frustrating for users who rely on this feature to convert their handwritten notes into digital text.

There are a few things you can do to improve the accuracy of the conversion process:

- **Make sure your handwriting is legible**. If the converter can't read your handwriting, it won't be able to convert it accurately.
- **Use simple language and short sentences**. The converter works best with simple language and short sentences. Avoid using abbreviations, acronyms, and jargon.
- **Use a pen with a narrow tip**. The converter works best with pens with narrow tips. Avoid using thick markers or highlighters.
- **Write on lined paper**. The converter works best when handwriting is written on lined paper. It helps the converter "read" the handwriting more accurately.

- **Take your time**. The converter works best when you take time and write slowly and clearly. Avoid writing in a hurry or in a sloppy way.

By following these tips, you can improve the accuracy of the conversion process and avoid losing or changing important information in your handwritten notes.

The Converted Text may not Match the Original Handwriting

If you're converting handwritten text to typed text in Numbers, there's a chance that the converted text may not perfectly match the original handwriting. The conversion process is imperfect, and some details may be lost in translation. However, the converted text should be accurate enough if you're looking for a general idea of the handwritten text.

Numbers Can Only Convert Handwriting to Text in English

When you convert handwriting to text in Numbers, the software can only accurately interpret and convert English text. The results may be inaccurate if you're trying to convert handwriting to another language - such as French or Spanish. The same is true for converting other languages' written characters into English text; the results may not be perfect.

CHAPTER 6: ADDING COLOR, GRADIENTS, AND IMAGES TO YOUR SPREADSHEETS

Color, gradients, and images are important design elements in Numbers. They can add visual interest and contrast to your documents, making them more engaging and visually appealing.

When incorporating color into your Numbers documents, remember a few things. First, consider the purpose of the document. Is it meant to be informational or decorative? If it's informational, you'll want to use colors that are easy to read and understand.

Second, think about the audience for the document. What types of colors will they respond best to? For example, corporate audiences may prefer more subdued colors, while creative audiences may prefer brighter, more vibrant colors.

Third, consider the overall design of the document. What colors will complement or contrast with the other elements in the document? For example, if you're using a lot of white space, you might want to use a dark color for your text to stand out. Or, if you're using many images, you might want to use a light color for your text so that it doesn't compete with the visuals.

You can also use color to convey meaning. For example, red might be used to indicate danger or urgency, while blue might be used to represent calmness or serenity. When using color in your document, be aware of the message you're trying to communicate and choose colors accordingly.

Gradients are another way to add visual interest to your Numbers documents. A gradient is a gradual transition from one color to another. You can create gradients using the built-in tools in Numbers or purchase pre-made gradient files to use in your documents.

When using gradients, keep in mind that you should use them sparingly. Too much of a gradient can make a document look busy or cluttered. Additionally, gradients can be difficult to read, so use them sparingly in text-heavy documents.

Images are another way to add visual interest to your Numbers documents. You can insert images from your computer or search for royalty-free images online.

When using images, keep in mind that you should use them sparingly. Too many images can make a document look busy or cluttered. Additionally, images can be difficult to read, so use them sparingly in text-heavy documents.

When incorporating color, gradients, and images into your Numbers documents, remember these tips to create engaging and visually appealing documents.

ADDING COLOR, GRADIENTS, AND IMAGES TO CELLS IN NUMBERS

In addition to adding text and numbers to cells, you can add color, gradients, and images. It can help make your data more visually appealing and easy to understand.

1. Select the cell or cells you want to format.
2. Click on the "Cell" tab in the Format sidebar.
3. To change the background color of the cell, click the "Fill" drop-down menu and select a color. You can also choose a gradient by selecting "Gradient Fill" and choosing a preset gradient or creating a custom one.
4. To add an image to the cell, click "Image Fill," then drag and drop an image onto the placeholder or click the "Choose" button to select an image from your files. You can also adjust the opacity and scale of the image using the options in the Image Fill section.
5. To add a border to the cell, click the "Border" drop-down menu and select a border style. You can adjust the line weight, color, and style of the border using the options in the Border section.
6. To apply the formatting to multiple cells, select the cells and click the "Paintbrush" button in the Format sidebar. Then click on the cell with the formatting you want to copy and click on the cells you want to apply it to.

APPLYING COLOR AND GRADIENT FILLS TO SHAPES IN NUMBERS

You can use color and gradient fills to add visual interest to shapes in Numbers.

1. First, select the shape you want to apply a fill to.
2. Next, click on the "Style" tab in the Format inspector.
3. From there, click on the "Fill" drop-down menu, and choose whether you want to apply a color or a gradient fill.
4. If you choose a color fill, you can either choose a preset color from the list or create a custom color by clicking on the color wheel.
5. If you choose a gradient fill, you can choose from several preset gradients or create a custom gradient by clicking on the gradient editor.
6. Once you've chosen the fill you want to apply, you can adjust the opacity and angle of the fill as desired.

By applying color and gradient fills to shapes in Numbers, you can make your spreadsheets more visually appealing and help to draw attention to important information.

INCORPORATING IMAGES INTO YOUR SPREADSHEET

Adding images to shapes in Numbers is a great way to add visual interest to your documents. Here's how:

1. Open the Numbers app on your Mac.
2. Click on the sheet that contains the shape you want to add an image to.
3. Select the shape by clicking on it.
4. From the "Inspector" panel, click on the "Graphic" tab.
5. In the "Fill" section, click on the "Image Fill" button.
6. Click on the "Choose" button and select the image file you want to use from your computer.
7. Adjust the image settings, such as the scale, position, and rotation, to fit the shape using the "Image Fill" section in the "Inspector" panel.
8. Click outside the shape to deselect it.

Once you have completed these steps, the image will be applied as a fill to the shape in your Numbers spreadsheet. By adding images to shapes, you can enhance the visual appeal of your spreadsheets and make them more engaging and informative.

ADJUSTING TRANSPARENCY AND RESIZING IMAGES

In Numbers, you can adjust the transparency and size of images to make them fit better into your spreadsheet. Here's how to do it:

Adjusting Transparency

1. First, select the image you want to adjust.
2. Click on the "Format" button in the upper-right corner of the Numbers window.
3. Click on the "Style" tab in the Format pane that appears.
4. Move the "Transparency" slider to the right to make the image more transparent, or to the left to make it less transparent.
5. Once you have set the desired level of transparency, you can close the Format pane.

Resizing Images

1. Select the image you want to resize.
2. Hover your mouse over one of the corners of the image until a double-headed arrow appears.
3. Click and drag the corner of the image to the desired size.
4. Alternatively, you can adjust the size of the image using the "Width" and "Height" fields in the "Arrange" tab of the Format pane.
5. Once you have set the desired size, you can close the Format pane.

Adjusting transparency and resizing images in Numbers can help you create more visually appealing and polished spreadsheets.

MODIFYING THE COLOR, GRADIENT, OR IMAGE OF A CELL IN NUMBERS

To modify the color, gradient, or image of a cell in Numbers, follow these steps:

1. Select the cell or cells that you want to modify.
2. In the format sidebar, click on the "Cell" tab.
3. To change the cell color, click the "Color Fill" drop-down menu and select a color. You can also use the color picker to select a custom color.
4. To apply a gradient to the cell, click the "Gradient Fill" drop-down menu and select a gradient. You can adjust the gradient direction and angle using the controls below the drop-down menu.
5. To add an image to the cell, click the "Image Fill" drop-down menu and select "Choose Image." Select an image from your files or drag and drop an image into the image well.
6. To adjust the transparency of the cell color, gradient, or image, use the "Opacity" slider under the fill options.
7. To remove the fill from the cell, select the cell and click the "No Fill" button in the format sidebar.

RESIZING AND MOVING CELLS

In Numbers, resizing and moving cells is a fundamental part of formatting and organizing your spreadsheet. Here are some steps to follow when resizing and moving cells:

Resizing Cells

1. Select the cells you want to resize. You can do this by clicking and dragging your mouse over the cells or by clicking on a specific cell and dragging the blue handle on the bottom right corner of the selection.
2. Once the cells are selected, hover your mouse over the border of the selected cells until you see a double arrow.
3. Click and drag the double arrow to resize the cells. You can resize both horizontally and vertically.

Moving Cells

1. Select the cells you want to move. You can do this by clicking and dragging your mouse over the cells or by clicking on a specific cell and dragging the blue handle on the bottom right corner of the selection.
2. Once the cells are selected, hover your mouse over the border of the selected cells until you see a four-arrow icon.
3. Click and drag the cells to their new location.

There are several keyboard shortcuts in Numbers that can be used for resizing and moving cells:

1. To move a cell or range of cells using the keyboard, first select the cells you want to move. Then, press and hold the "Option" key and use the arrow keys to move the cells in the desired direction.
2. To resize a cell or range of cells using the keyboard, first select the cells you want to resize. Then, press and hold the "Option" and "Shift" keys simultaneously. Use the arrow keys to increase or decrease the size of the cells.
3. To quickly resize a single column or row, click on the header for the column or row you want to resize. Then, press and hold the "Option" key while dragging the header to the desired size.

DELETING COLOR, GRADIENTS, AND IMAGES FROM CELLS IN NUMBERS

If you're no longer happy with the color, gradient, or image you've applied to a cell in Numbers, you can delete it by following these steps:

1. Tap the cell that contains the color, gradient, or image you want to remove.
2. In the Format sidebar, tap the Cell tab.
3. Tap the drop-down menu next to Fill and select None.
4. Tap Done to save your changes.

TROUBLESHOOTING COMMON IMAGE ISSUES

If your color, gradient, or image doesn't appear the way you expect it to in Numbers, there are a few things you can try.

First, check that your document is using the correct color profile. To do this, go to the Inspector's Document tab and ensure the Color Profile drop-down menu is set to sRGB IEC61966-2.1.

If that doesn't fix the problem, try resetting your document's colors by clicking the Document tab in the Inspector and the Reset Colors button.

If you're still having trouble, make sure that the image you're using is in an RGB color space. You can check this by opening the image in an image editing program like Photoshop and looking at the color mode. It should say RGB.

If you're still having trouble after that, try creating a new document and importing your color, gradient, or image. It will often fix any problems caused by corrupt or incompatible data.

You can also delete colors, gradients, and images from cells by selecting them and pressing the Delete key on your keyboard.

One of the most common issues people have with Numbers is getting colors, gradients, and images to display correctly in cells.

- Make sure the cell is big enough to accommodate the content. Sometimes increasing the height or width of the cell can help.
- If the cell has a lot of content, try adjusting the font size or line spacing. It can help make the content more readable.
- Make sure that the color profile of your document is set to "RGB Color" or "Generic RGB." You can change this in the "Document Info" section of the Numbers app.

CHAPTER 7: WORKING WITH SHAPES IN NUMBERS

Shapes play an essential role in the Numbers app. They help to create a visual representation of data, making it easier to understand and interpret. There are a variety of shapes available to use, each with its purpose and meaning. By understanding the different roles that shapes can play, you'll be able to use them more effectively to communicate your data.

One of the most basic uses for shapes is simply delineating different data areas. For example, you might use a rectangle to surround a group of cells representing one data category and use a different shape to surround another group representing a different category. It can help to visually separate the two data sets, making understanding the relationships between them easier.

You can also use shapes to highlight specific data points. For example, you might use a larger or brighter-colored shape to draw attention to a crucial data point. It can help ensure that your audience doesn't miss anything important.

Finally, you can use shapes to add a bit of visual interest to your Numbers document. It can help to make it more visually appealing and can also help to keep your audience engaged.

When using shapes in the Numbers app, they must remember their purpose and meaning. Doing so will allow you to use them more effectively to communicate your data.

HOW TO INSERT A SHAPE IN NUMBERS

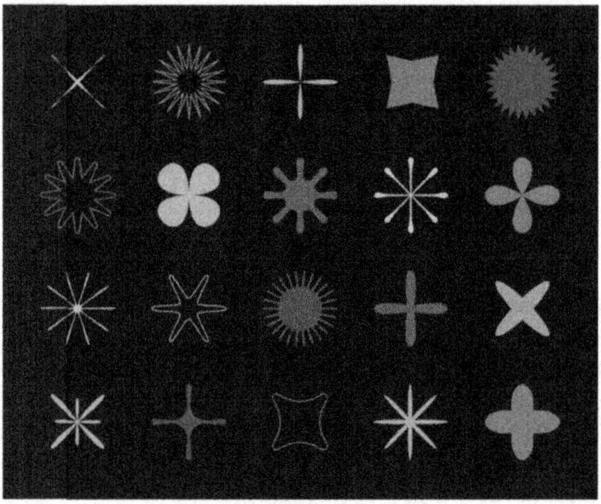

To insert a shape in Numbers, follow these steps:

1. Tap the "+" sign at the top-right corner of the screen.
2. Select "Shape" from the menu that appears.
3. Choose the type of shape you want to insert from the options that appear.
4. Tap and drag your finger to place the shape where you want it on the screen.
5. Tap "Done" when you're finished.

HOW TO CHANGE THE COLOR OF A SHAPE IN NUMBERS

To change the color of a shape in Numbers, do the following:

1. Select the shape you want to change.
2. In the "Format" panel, click on the "Fill" tab.
3. Choose the color you want from the palette.
4. Click "OK" to save your changes.

You can also change the color of a shape by selecting it and then clicking on the "Fill" color swatch in the "Format" panel. It will open the color picker, where you can choose a new color. Click "OK" to save your changes.

HOW TO DELETE A SHAPE

The first way is to select the shape and press the "delete" button on your keyboard. You can right-click or two-finger tap on the shape and select "delete" from the menu that appears as well.

If you want to delete multiple shapes at once, you can select them all. While clicking on each shape, simply hold down the "shift" key. Then, you can press the "delete" button or right-click and select "delete" from the menu.

You can also delete a shape by selecting it and then clicking on the trashcan icon at the screen's top.

UTILIZING THE SHAPES LIBRARY ON MOBILE DEVICES

To use shapes in Numbers on an iPhone or iPad, select the cell you want to insert a shape into. Then tap the "Shapes" icon in the toolbar at the top of the screen.

It will open up the shapes library, which contains various shapes you can insert into your spreadsheet. To insert a shape, tap on it.

You can also resize and move shapes after they've been inserted by tapping on them and then using the handles that appear. And if you need to delete a shape, tap on it and then hit the "Delete" button.

That's all there is to using shapes in Numbers! With this handy tool, you can make your spreadsheets much more visually appealing and easier to understand. So, experiment with different shapes to see what works best for your needs.

CHAPTER 8: UNDERSTANDING FUNCTIONS IN NUMBERS

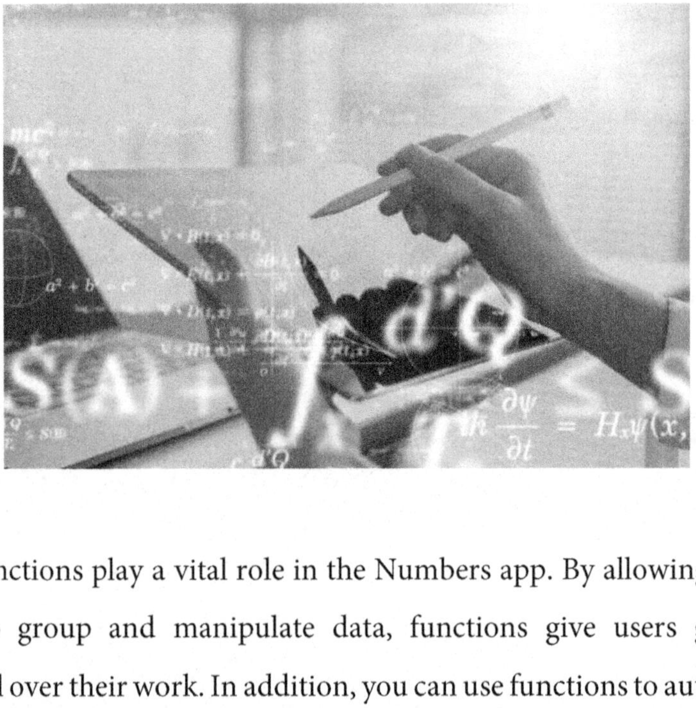

Functions play a vital role in the Numbers app. By allowing users to group and manipulate data, functions give users greater control over their work. In addition, you can use functions to automate tasks, making it easier and faster to complete work.

Whether you are looking to organize your data or automate a task, the Numbers app has a function that can help. To learn more about the role of functions in Numbers, read on.

As previously mentioned, you can use functions to sort and manipulate data. It is done by creating a function formula, which is then applied to a range of cells. For example, you could use a function to sum a column of numbers or count the number of cells that contain a certain value.

You can also use functions to automate tasks. For example, you could use a function to automatically insert the current date into a cell or calculate the average of a range of cells. By automating tasks, you can save time and reduce errors.

Although functions are immensely powerful, they are not always necessary. Sometimes, completing a task may be easier and faster without a function. For example, if you only need to sum a column of numbers once, you may not need to create a function formula.

When deciding to use a function, consider the following:

- How often will the task be completed? If the task is going to be completed once, a function may not be necessary.
- How complex is the task? If the task is quite simple, a function may not be necessary.
- How much time do you have to complete the task? A function may not be necessary if you only have a few minutes to complete the task.

In general, functions should be used when they will save time or reduce errors. When in doubt, err on the side of using a function. The role of functions in Numbers is to save time and reduce errors. When deciding about using a function, consider the task at hand and how you could complete it more efficiently with a function.

TYPES OF FUNCTIONS

There are many types of functions in the Numbers app. You can use these functions to perform mathematical operations, convert units, and more. Here are some common types of functions in Numbers app:

- Basic Math Functions: These functions are used for simple math calculations and include addition (+), subtraction (-), multiplication (*), and division (/).
- Statistical Functions: These functions are used to analyze and summarize large sets of data and include functions like SUM, AVERAGE, MEDIAN, and MODE.
- Financial Functions: These functions are used to perform financial calculations and include functions like PV (present value), FV (future value), NPV (net present value), and IRR (internal rate of return).
- Date and Time Functions: These functions are used to manipulate and analyze dates and times and include functions like NOW, TODAY, MONTH, and YEAR.

- Text Functions: These functions are used to manipulate and format text and include functions like CONCATENATE, LEFT, RIGHT, and MID.
- Lookup and Reference Functions: These functions are used to search and reference data in a table or range of cells and include functions like VLOOKUP, HLOOKUP, INDEX, and MATCH.
- Logical Functions: These functions are used to evaluate logical expressions and include functions like IF, AND, OR, and NOT.
- Engineering Functions: These functions are used for complex engineering calculations and include functions like CONVERT, ABS, and SQRT.

To use a function in Numbers, you typically type the function name followed by its arguments. For example, to add two numbers, you can use the SUM function and type "=SUM(5, 10)" into a cell.

For conversion functions, like "CONVERT(mi, km)", you would specify the value you want to convert and the units you want to convert from and to. For example, to convert 10 miles to kilometers, you would use the CONVERT function and type "=CONVERT(10, "mi", "km")" into a cell.

You can find a full list of functions in the Numbers app by tapping the "Functions" button in the toolbar. It will open up a menu with all of the available functions. Tap on the function you want to use and enter the values you want to use.

USING FUNCTIONS IN NUMBERS FORMULAS

Functions are a powerful tool in Numbers that allow you to perform calculations and operations on your data. To use functions in Numbers formulas, follow these steps:

1. Select the cell where you want to enter your formula.
2. Begin your formula with an equal sign (=).
3. Type the name of the function you want to use, followed by an open parenthesis.
4. Enter the arguments for the function, separated by commas. The arguments are the values that the function will operate on.
5. Close the parenthesis and press Enter to complete the formula.

Here are some examples of common functions and their syntax:

1. SUM: Adds a range of numbers. Syntax: =SUM(number1:number2)
2. AVERAGE: Calculates the average of a range of numbers. Syntax: =AVERAGE(number1:number2)
3. COUNT: Counts the number of cells in a range that contain numerical data. Syntax: =COUNT(range)

Example: Suppose you have a spreadsheet that contains a list of products sold in a store, and you want to know how many of these products cost more than $50. You can use the COUNT function to count the number of cells in a given range that contain values greater than $50.

1) First, select a blank cell where you want to display the count result.
2) Then, enter the COUNT function by typing "=COUNT(" in the cell.
3) Now, select the range of cells that contain the product prices.
4) Enter the condition for the COUNT function, in this case ">50".
5) Close the parentheses and press Enter.

The formula will look something like this: =COUNT(A2:A10,">50")

This will count the number of cells in the range A2 to A10 that contain values greater than $50.

4. MAX: Returns the maximum value in a range of numbers.
   Syntax: =MAX(number1:number2)

Example: Suppose you have a list of numbers in cells A1 through A10, and you want to find the highest value in that range. You can use the MAX function to do this. Simply select an empty cell (let's say B1) and enter the following formula:

1) =MAX(A1:A10)

This formula tells Numbers to find the highest value in the range A1 to A10 and display it in cell B1. If the highest value is in cell A3 (let's say the value is 100), then cell B1 will display "100".

5. MIN: Returns the minimum value in a range of numbers. Syntax: =MIN(number1:number2)

Example: Let's say we have a table of sales data, with the total sales for each month in a column. We can use the MIN function to find the lowest sales number for the year. Here's how:

1) Select the cell where you want the result to appear.
2) Type "=MIN(" (without the quotes) into the cell.
3) Select the range of cells you want to find the minimum value for. In this case, we would select the column with the sales data.
4) Type ")" (without the quotes) and press Enter.

6. IF: Evaluates a condition and returns one value if the condition is true and another value if it is false. Syntax: =IF(condition, value_if_true, value_if_false).

Example: Suppose you have a list of test scores for a group of students, and you want to flag any scores that are below a certain threshold. You could use the IF function to create a new column that indicates whether each score is "Pass" or "Fail".

1) First, create a new column next to the column containing the test scores. You can do this by right-clicking on the column header and selecting "Insert Left" or "Insert Right".
2) In the first cell of the new column, type the following formula:

3) =IF(B2>=70,"Pass","Fail") This formula checks the value in cell B2 (assuming that's where the first test score is) and returns "Pass" if the score is 70 or higher, and "Fail" if it's below 70.
4) Copy the formula down the entire column to apply it to all of the test scores.

By using these and other functions, you can perform complex calculations and manipulate your data in a variety of ways. Remember to always check the syntax of a function to ensure that you are using it correctly.

CHAPTER 9: PRECISE OBJECT EDITING

Precise object editing in Numbers is a great way to ensure that your data is accurate and up-to-date. You can use it to edit objects such as cells, ranges, columns, and rows. Precise object editing can help you correct errors in your data or add new information.

When you intend to precise the object edit in Numbers, you can select the object you want to edit. It can be helpful if you need to make a small change to your data or if you want to add new information. For example, if you wanted to add a new row of data, you could use precise object editing to select the cells in the row and then enter the new data.

Precise object editing can also be helpful when you are working with large amounts of data. If you need to change many cells, you can use precise object editing to select all the cells you want to change. It can save you time and ensure that you don't accidentally make changes to other cells in your data.

If you are working with sensitive data, precise object editing can help you protect your information. You can use it to select the cells that contain sensitive data and then lock them. It will prevent others from being able to view or change the data in those cells.

Precise object editing is a powerful tool to help you manage your data more effectively. You can use it to make small changes or add new information. You can also use it to protect sensitive data. If you are not already using precise object editing in Numbers, you should consider doing so. It can save you time and ensure that your data is accurate and up-to-date.

HOW TO USE PRECISE OBJECT EDITING

With Precise object editing in Numbers, you can quickly and easily adjust the size, shape, and position of objects on your canvas. This feature is handy when working with complex designs or laying out pages for Print.

To use Precise object editing:

1. First, select the object you want to edit. You can select an object by clicking on it or by using the Shift key to select multiple objects.
2. Once you've selected your object, go to the "Format" tab in the Numbers toolbar. Here, you will see a section called "Object Styles." Click on the arrow next to "Object Styles" to open a drop-down menu.
3. From the drop-down menu, select "More." This will open the "Style" window.
4. In the "Style" window, you will see a variety of options for editing your object, including "Layout," "Borders," "Shadow," and "Reflection." You can use these options to customize the appearance of your object.
5. To make precise edits to your object, click on the "Size and Position" tab in the "Style" window. Here, you will see options for adjusting the object's position, size, rotation, and scale.
6. Use the sliders and input fields to make precise adjustments to your object. You can also use the arrow keys on your keyboard to make small adjustments to the object's position and size.
7. Once you're happy with your changes, click "OK" to apply the new styles to your object.

When you're working with objects in Precise object editing mode, you can also use the following features:

- **Duplicate an object:** Tap the Duplicate button, then tap the duplicate object to move it.
- **Delete an object:** Tap the Delete button.
- **Bring an object forward or send it backward:** Tap the Arrange button and then Bring Forward or Send Backward.
- **Lock an object in place:** Tap the Lock button. Locked objects can't be moved or edited.
- **Group multiple objects:** Tap the Group button, then tap the objects you want to group. To Ungroup objects, tap the Ungroup button.

Precise object editing is a great way to fine-tune your designs in Numbers. Give it a try the next time you're working on a complex project!

ACCESSING THE PRECISE OBJECT EDITING IN NUMBERS

To access the Precise Object Editing feature in Numbers, follow these steps:

1. Open the Numbers app and create or open a document containing an object that you want to edit.
2. Select the object by clicking on it once. The object will be surrounded by a blue outline when it is selected.
3. With the object still selected, click on the "Arrange" button in the top-right corner of the window.
4. In the drop-down menu that appears, select "Precise Object Editing" near the bottom of the list.

You can also adjust the object's position and size numerically by entering values into the Inspector pane on the right-hand side of the screen. To do this, click on the "Inspector" button in the top-right corner of the window, and then select the "Metrics" tab. Here, you can enter precise measurements for the object's size, position, and rotation.

CHAPTER 10: CREATING CAPTIONS AND TITLES

There are two types of text in Numbers: captions and titles. Captions are the labels you see on the left side of the interface, such as "Name" or "Total." Titles are headers at the top of each column, such as "January" or "Q1."

You can add or edit captions and titles by double-clicking on them. It will open up a text editor where you can make your changes.

There are a few things to keep in mind when working with captions and titles:

- Captions are typically used for labeling data, while titles are used for organizing data.
- You can use both captions and titles to sort and filter your data.
- Captions and titles can be different lengths, but they will always be the same width on the screen.
- You can use HTML tags in captions and titles to format your text. For example, you can use the <b> tag to make the text bold or the <i> tag to make the text italic.

In general, it's a good idea to keep your captions and titles short so they're easy to read.

ADDING CAPTIONS AND TITLES

Adding captions and titles to your Numbers spreadsheets can help organize and present your data clearly and professionally. Plus, it can make working with large amounts of data much easier. Here's how to add captions and titles in Numbers:

1. First, select the cell where you want to add the caption or title.
2. Next, click on the "Cell" tab in the top menu, and then select "Table" from the dropdown menu.

3. From the Table menu, select "Add Header Row" or "Add Footer Row," depending on where you want your caption or title to appear.
4. Once you've added the header or footer row, you can type in your caption or title. You can also format the text to make it more readable by selecting it and using the formatting options in the top menu.
5. If you want to add an image to your caption or title, click on the "Media" button in the top menu and select "Choose." From there, you can select an image from your computer or other device.
6. Click "OK."

Your caption or title will now appear above or below your selected cells.

EDITING CAPTIONS AND TITLES

If you're working with a Numbers spreadsheet that contains a lot of data, you may want to edit the captions and titles to make the data more easily understandable. Here's how:

1. Select the cell that you intend to edit.
2. Click the "Edit" button in the toolbar.
3. Click the "Captions & Titles" button in the editing menu.
4. Make your changes in the "Captions & Titles" dialogue box.
5. Click the "OK" button to save your changes.

You can also format your captions and titles using the "Captions & Titles" dialogue box. To do this, select the cells you want to format and click the "Format" button in the dialogue box. You can choose how you want your captions and titles to be formatted.

Captions and titles can be a great way to make your Numbers spreadsheets more understandable. By editing them, you can ensure that your data is easy to read and comprehend.

DELETING CAPTIONS AND TITLES

To delete a caption or title in Numbers:

1. Click on the text box containing the caption or title you want to delete.
2. Press the Delete key on your keyboard or right-click on the text box and select "Delete" from the context menu.
3. If you want to delete all captions or titles in your document, use the "Find" and "Replace" feature to search for the specific text and delete it.

Note: If you want to temporarily hide a caption or title without deleting it, you can simply select the text box and press the "H" key on your keyboard to hide it. To unhide the text, press "H" again.

CHAPTER 11: INCORPORATING AUDIO INTO YOUR SPREADSHEETS

Adding audio to Numbers can help bring your data to life and make it more engaging for your audience. Audio can also be a great way to add accessibility for those who may not be able to see your data or who prefer to listen rather than read.

WAYS TO ADD AUDIO

There are several ways to add audio to your spreadsheets in Numbers. One way is to use the Media Browser. You can find the Media Browser in the toolbar at the top of the Numbers window. To use the Media Browser, simply drag and drop an audio file into your document. The Media Browser will automatically insert the audio file into your document.

Another way to add audio is to use the Audio Recorder. To access this feature, select the cell where you want to add the audio and click the "Audio" button in the toolbar. From there, you can choose to record audio using your computer's microphone. Once you've finished recording, the audio will be inserted into your document.

The third way to add audio is to use the Audio Inspector. The Audio Inspector can be found in the toolbar at the top of the Numbers window. To use it, select an audio file in your document and click on the Inspector button in the toolbar. You'll see options for playback, volume, and looping in the Inspector window.

Adding audio to your spreadsheets can help make them more engaging and accessible for your audience. Whether you choose to use the Media Browser, Audio Recorder, or Audio Inspector, adding audio is a simple process in Numbers.

ADDING AUDIO TO YOUR NUMBERS SPREADSHEET

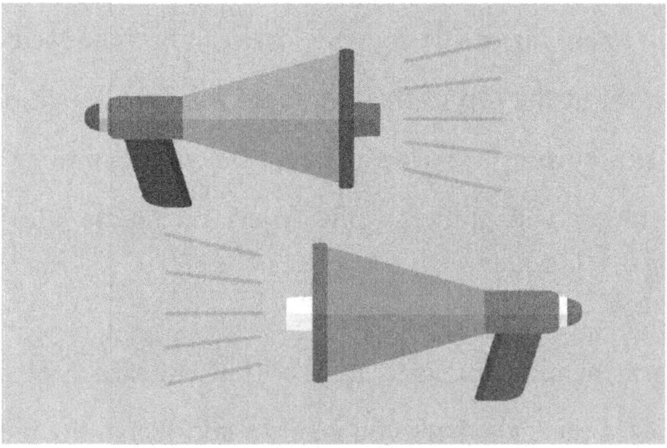

You can add audio to your Numbers spreadsheet by inserting an audio file from your computer or using the built-in microphone to record audio directly into the spreadsheet.

To Insert an Audio File:

1. Click on the cell where you want to insert the audio file.
2. Click the Insert menu and select audio.
3. Select the audio file you intend to insert and click Open.
4. You will then insert the audio file into the spreadsheet.

To record audio directly into the spreadsheet:

1. Click on the cell where you want to insert the audio recording.
2. Click the Insert menu and select audio.
3. Click the Record button.

4. Start speaking into the microphone.
5. Select the Stop button once you're done recording.
6. You will then insert the Audio Recording into the spreadsheet.

HOW TO ADD AN AUDIO FILE FROM YOUR COMPUTER IN NUMBERS

1. Click on the cell where you want to insert the audio file.
2. Go to the "Insert" menu at the top of the screen.
3. Select "Audio" from the dropdown menu.
4. In the file browser window that appears, navigate to the location of the audio file you want to insert and select it.
5. Click "Open" to insert the audio file into the selected cell.

HOW TO ADD AN AUDIO FILE FROM THE WEB

To add an audio file from the web in Numbers, first, open the Numbers app and click on the Media Browser icon in the toolbar. In the Media Browser window, select the Audio tab and search for the audio file you want to add. Once you find the audio file, click on it and then click on the "Add" button. This will add the audio file to your Numbers document.

To listen to the audio file, click on the "Play" button, or right-click on the audio file and select "save as" to download it to your computer. You can also add the audio file to your iTunes library to listen to it on your iPod or iPhone. With these simple steps, you can easily add audio files from the web to your Numbers spreadsheets.

HOW TO ADD AN AUDIO FILE FROM YOUR IOS DEVICE

Audio files from your iOS device can be added to Numbers spreadsheets in two ways: via the media browser or by using the share sheet.

To add an audio file from the media browser:

1. Tap the "+" button at the screen's top-left corner.
2. Select "Media" from the list of options.
3. Tap "Audio" in the media browser.
4. Select the audio file you wish to add.

To add an audio file using the share sheet:

1. Tap the "+" button at the top-left corner of the screen.
2. Select "Share Sheet" from the list of options.
3. Tap "Audio" in the share sheet.
4. Select the audio file you wish to add.

Adding audio files from your iOS device is a great way to enhance your Numbers spreadsheets. Whether you're adding sound effects to a game or want to include a musical accompaniment, audio files can add an extra level of interest and engagement.

HOW TO RECORD AN AUDIO FILE IN NUMBERS

Now that you know how to set up your audio recording device in Numbers, it's time to learn how to record an audio file.

1. To record an audio file in Numbers, open the Audio Recorder window by clicking on the "Audio Recorder" button in the toolbar.
2. First, ensure that the "Input" drop-down menu is set to the audio input device you want to use. Afterward, select the "Record" button to start recording.
3. You can stop recording anytime by clicking on the "Stop" button. Once you're finished recording, you can click on the "Play" button to listen back to your recording.

That's all there is to it! Now you know how to record an audio file in Numbers.

HOW TO EDIT AN AUDIO FILE

If you have an audio file you need to edit, there are a few different ways you can do so in Numbers. Here's a look at how to get started:

1. Open the Numbers file that contains the audio file.
2. Select the audio file by clicking on it once.
3. Select the "Edit" button in the toolbar.
4. Make your edits to the audio file.
5. Click on the "Save" button to save your changes.

HOW TO DELETE AN AUDIO FILE

Deleting an audio file from Numbers is simple. Just follow these steps:

1. Open the Numbers document that contains the audio file you want to delete.
2. Select the audio file by clicking on it once.
3. Press the "Delete" key on your keyboard. The audio file will be deleted from the Numbers document.

CHAPTER 12: CUSTOM TEMPLATES IN NUMBERS

Numbers offers a wide variety of custom templates that you can use to create beautiful spreadsheets. Whether you need to track your finances, manage a small business, or keep tabs on a large corporation, there's a Numbers template to suit your needs.

To find the perfect template for your needs, browse the available options. You can filter templates by category or search for a specific template by name.

If you're satisfied with the template, download it and start entering your information. Numbers make it easy to input data, add formulas, and customize the appearance of your spreadsheet. With a little effort, you can create a professional-looking document that will impress your boss or clients.

So, what are you waiting for? Start browsing Numbers templates today and see how easy it is to create beautiful spreadsheets in Numbers.

CREATING A CUSTOM TEMPLATE

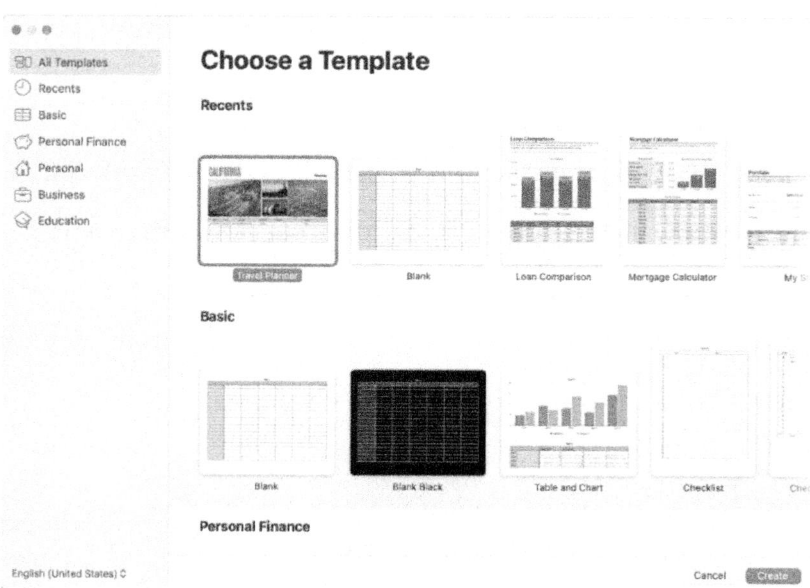

Creating a custom template in Numbers is easy and only requires a few simple steps. Here's how you can create your own custom template in Numbers:

1. Open Numbers on your Mac.
2. Click on the "File" menu in the top left corner of the screen and select "New Template".
3. Choose the type of template you want to create, such as a "Blank" or "Personal Budget" template.
4. Customize the template to fit your needs by adding tables, charts, and text boxes.
5. Once you've finished creating your template, click on the "File" menu and select "Save as Template".
6. Enter a name for your custom template and click "Save".

Your custom template will now be saved and accessible from the "My Templates" section of the template chooser.

Creating a custom template in Numbers can save you time and make your workflow more efficient. By customizing your own template, you can ensure that your spreadsheets are always set up the way you need them to be.

SAVING A CUSTOM TEMPLATE IN NUMBERS

If you've created a custom template in Numbers that you want to save for future use, follow these steps.

1. Select the template you want to save from the Template Chooser.
2. Click the Save as Template button in the lower-left corner of the Template Chooser.
3. Enter a name for your template, then click Save.

It will now save your custom template in the My Templates section of the Template Chooser for future use.

ACCESSING CUSTOM TEMPLATES

Select the "Templates" tab from the Numbers home screen to access custom templates in Numbers. You can browse through a selection of custom templates or search for a specific template by keyword. Once you've found the perfect template for your needs, click on it to open it up in the Numbers interface.

You can also access custom templates in Numbers by selecting "File" > "New from Template..." from the menu bar. It will open a Finder window where you can browse your template library. Select the template you want to use and click "Open" to open it in Numbers.

EDITING A CUSTOM TEMPLATE

Once you've created a custom template in Numbers, you can edit it to change the look and feel of your document. To edit a custom template:

1. Open Numbers and select the template you want to edit from the Templates browser.
2. Click the Edit button in the toolbar.
3. Make changes to the template, such as adding or removing elements, changing colors or fonts, etc.
4. When you're finished, click the Save button in the toolbar.

Your changes will be saved to the template and will be applied to any new documents created from it. If you want to revert to the original version of the template, you can click the Revert to Original button in the toolbar.

DELETING A CUSTOM TEMPLATE

1. In the Numbers app, open the spreadsheet that contains the custom template you want to delete.
2. Tap the "More" button in the top-right corner of the screen.
3. Scroll down and tap "Manage Custom Templates."
4. Tap the "Delete" button next to the template you want to delete.
5. Tap "Delete Template" to confirm.

Custom templates can be a great way to save time when creating new documents in Numbers. However, if you no longer need a particular template, you can delete it from your library using the steps described above. It will ensure that your template library only contains the templates you need.

CHAPTER 13: MISCELLANEOUS FEATURES

Numbers has a number of miscellaneous features that allow you to work with a variety of file formats, import images, and add files to your spreadsheet. Here are some of the key features:

1. **Importing files:** You can import Microsoft Excel spreadsheets, Comma Separated Values (CSV), and tab-delimited text files into Numbers from your Mac or a Windows PC. You can also import Numbers '09 spreadsheets, CSV files, and tab-delimited text files on an iPad.

2. **Editing Excel files:** You can open a Numbers spreadsheet in Excel and edit it like any other Excel file. To do this, open the Numbers spreadsheet in Numbers, then choose File > Export To > Microsoft Excel.
3. **Converting to other file formats:** If you want to edit the Numbers spreadsheet in another application, such as Google Sheets, you can first convert it to a different file format. To do this, open the Numbers spreadsheet in Numbers, choose File > Export To > CSV, and then open the CSV file in the other application. You can also import Apple Pages, Microsoft Word, and Rich Text Format (RTF) files into Numbers on a Mac. To do this, open the document in the other application, choose File > Export To > Numbers, and then open the file in Numbers. Using Numbers on an iPad, you can also import Apple Pages documents and Rich Text Format (RTF) files. To do this, open the document in the other application, choose File > Share > Send Copy As PDF, and then open the file in Numbers.
4. **Importing images:** You can import photos and images from your Photos library or another app, such as Google Drive or Dropbox. To do this, open the image in the other app, choose File > Share > Send Copy As PDF, and then open the file in Numbers. You can add images to a Numbers spreadsheet by dragging them from the Photos app or another app into a cell.

To do this, touch and hold the image until the menu appears, then drag the image to the cell.

5. **Adding files:** Using Numbers on a Mac, you can add files from your iCloud Drive or another cloud storage service, such as Google Drive or Dropbox. To do this, open the file in the other app, choose File > Share > Send Copy As PDF, and then open the file in Numbers. If you're using Numbers on an iPad, you can add files from iCloud Drive or another cloud storage service by opening the file in the other app, choosing File > Share > Send Copy As PDF, and then opening the file in Numbers. You can add files to a Numbers spreadsheet by dragging them into a cell from the iCloud Drive app or another app. To do this, touch and hold the file until the menu appears, then drag the file to the cell.

With these miscellaneous features, Numbers allows you to work with a variety of file formats and import images and files, making it a versatile tool for creating and managing spreadsheets.

CHAPTER 14: BENEFITS OF USING NUMBERS FOR BEGINNERS

If you're new to the Numbers app for Apple, you may be wondering what all the fuss is about. After all, there are plenty of other spreadsheet apps out there. So, what makes Numbers stand out?

Here are some benefits that Numbers offer:

EASE OF USE AND VERSATILITY

Several things make the Number App for Apple easy to use. First, it is straightforward to navigate. The interface is uncluttered and clean, so you won't be overwhelmed with options or features. Second, the app provides clear instructions on how to use its various features. And third, it offers a variety of helpful tutorials that show you how to get the most out of the app.

Overall, if you're searching for a simple-to-use app to keep you organized and on top of your finances, the Number App for Apple is a great option.

The Numbers App for Apple is a versatile tool for various purposes. Whether you need to quickly add up a bill, calculate the tip at a restaurant, or calculate the amount of change you should receive after purchasing an item - this app can do it all! It can be used for various chores, from tracking your finances to creating a budget, organizing your schedule, and managing a project.

COMPATIBILITY WITH OTHER APPLE PRODUCTS

If you're already using other Apple products like the iPhone and iPad, you'll be pleased to know that Numbers is compatible with them.

It means you can easily share files and data between your devices.

UNIQUE FEATURES AND AFFORDABILITY

Despite its simplicity, Numbers is still a powerful spreadsheet app. It includes every capability you might possibly need to do the task, including support for complex formulas, data visualization tools, and more.

Numbers are worth considering if you're looking for a budget-friendly option. It's much cheaper than comparable apps like Microsoft Excel, yet it still offers all the features you need to get the job done.

GREAT FOR BEGINNERS

The Numbers app for Apple is an excellent tool for beginners who want to manage their finances. Using it makes it easy to track your spending, budget for upcoming expenses, and see where your money goes each month. You can also use the Numbers app to create charts and graphs to visualize your financial data. The best part about the Numbers app is that it's free to download and use.

HANDLING FINANCES

The Numbers app for Apple is an excellent option if you're looking for a better way to handle your finances. Numbers can help you track your spending, budget for upcoming expenses, and see where your money goes each month. Plus, the Numbers app makes it easy to create charts and graphs to visualize your financial data. And best of all, the Numbers app is free to download and use.

Whether a complete beginner or a seasoned pro, Numbers is an excellent option for anyone needing a powerful and versatile spreadsheet app.

CHAPTER 15: TIPS FOR EFFECTIVE USE OF NUMBERS

You can do a few things to ensure you use the Numbers App for Apple effectively. Here are some tips:

USE TEMPLATES

When you open the Numbers app, you'll see a variety of templates to choose from. Beautiful spreadsheets can be quickly created using these templates. To use a template, tap on it and then enter your data. The template will automatically format everything for you.

There are templates for various purposes, including budgets, invoices, and more. And if you can't find what you're looking for, you can always create your custom template.

ORGANIZE YOUR DATA

Sort your data based on what makes sense to you. This will make it easier to find and use when you need it.

USE KEYBOARD SHORTCUTS

This can help you work more efficiently by reducing the need to constantly switch between the mouse and keyboard. For example, you can use shortcuts to quickly insert rows or columns, or to apply formatting to cells.

Here are few shortcuts:

- Command-N: Create a new spreadsheet.
- Command-O: Open an existing spreadsheet.
- Command-S: Save the current spreadsheet.
- Command-P: Print the current spreadsheet.
- Command-F: Search within the current spreadsheet.
- Command-Z: Undo the last action.
- Command-Y: Redo the last undone action.
- Command-X: Cut the selected cells, rows, or columns.

- Command-C: Copy the selected cells, rows, or columns.
- Command-V: Paste the cut or copied cells, rows, or columns.
- Command-A: Select all cells in the current spreadsheet.
- Command-B: Bold the selected text.
- Command-I: Italicize the selected text.
- Command-U: Underline the selected text.
- Command-T: Open the Fonts panel to format the selected text.
- Command-1: Open the Format panel to format the selected cells, rows, or columns.
- Command-2: Open the Table panel to format the current table.
- Command-3: Open the Chart panel to format the current chart.
- Command-4: Open the Inspector to customize object properties.
- Command-5: Show or hide the Media browser.
- Command-6: Show or hide the Comments pane.
- Command-7: Show or hide the Table of Contents pane.
- Command-8: Show or hide the Layout pane.
- Command-9: Show or hide the Find and Replace pane.
- Control-Tab: Switch between open spreadsheets.

USE FORMULAS

The app includes a variety of built-in formulas that you can use to perform calculations on your data. Be sure to take advantage of this feature to save time and energy.

USE CHARTS AND GRAPHS

The app also includes several built-in charts and graphs that you can use to visualize your data. Understanding trends and identifying relationships between different data points can be helpful.

SHARE YOUR WORK

The app includes several options to share your work with others. It can be helpful if you're working on a project collaboratively or want to share your results with others.

These pointers will aid you in getting the most out of the Numbers App for Apple and following them will make your experience with the app more efficient and effective.

CONCLUSION

The Numbers app from Apple is a powerful tool for managing data and performing calculations. With its easy-to-use interface, you can quickly input data and perform various mathematical operations. In addition, the app provides a wide range of features that allow you to customize your experience. Whether you're looking to create simple spreadsheets or complex financial models, the Numbers app can help you get the job done.

The Numbers app makes it easy to input data into your spreadsheet. To do so, tap on a cell and start typing. Also, you can use the app's built-in keyboard shortcuts to enter data quickly. For example, pressing the "Tab" key will move you to the next cell, while pressing "Enter" will create a new row.

After entering your data, you can use the Numbers app to perform various calculations. To do so, tap on a cell and select the "Formula" option. You can choose from various pre-defined formulas or create your custom ones. Once you have entered your formula, the app will automatically calculate the results and display them in the cell.

The Numbers app provides several features that allow you to customize your experience. For example, you can change the cells' font, size, and color to better suit your needs. You can add images and charts to your spreadsheet to make it visually appealing. In addition, the app provides several templates that you can use to create professional-looking spreadsheets quickly.

Whether you're looking to create simple spreadsheets or complex financial models, the Numbers app from Apple can help you get the job done. With its easy-to-use interface and excellent features, you'll be able to input data, perform calculations, and customize your experience to suit your needs more.

To conclude, the Numbers app for Apple is an excellent tool for managing and analyzing data. It is easy to use and has various features that make it a valuable asset for businesses and individuals. The Numbers app is worth considering if you are looking for a reliable and user-friendly app to help with all your data management needs.

Printed in Great Britain
by Amazon

60652574R00070